Can You

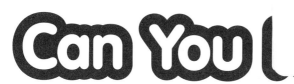

by Quinn Baker
illustrated by Sue Williams

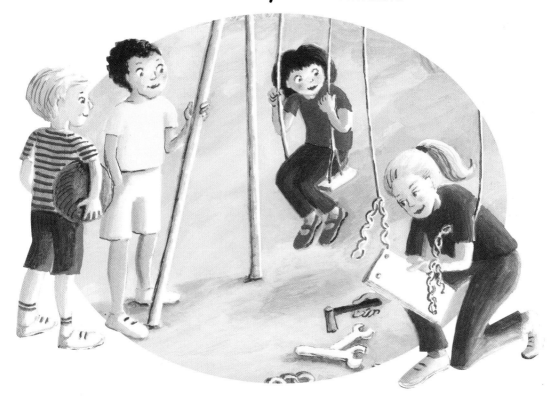

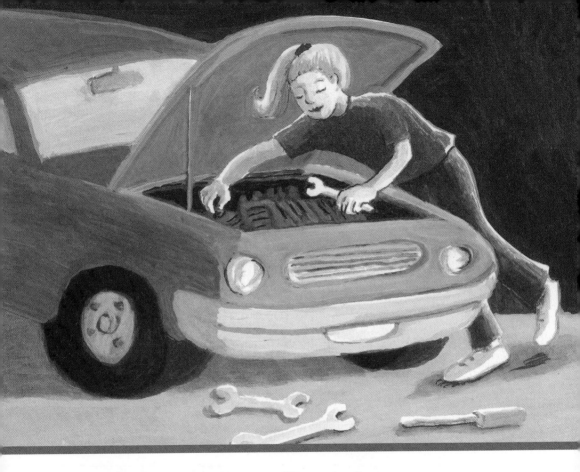

You can fix the car.

2

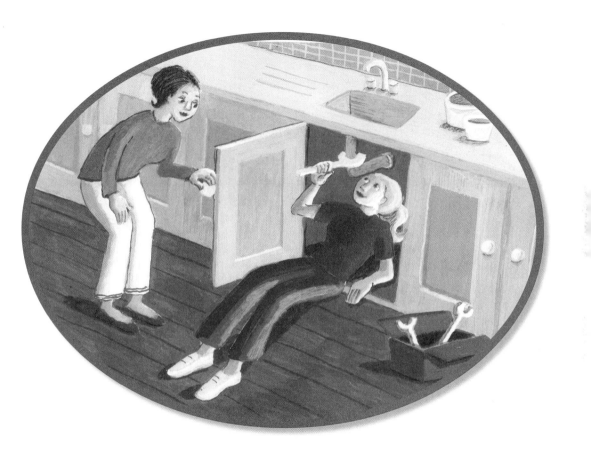

You can fix the sink.

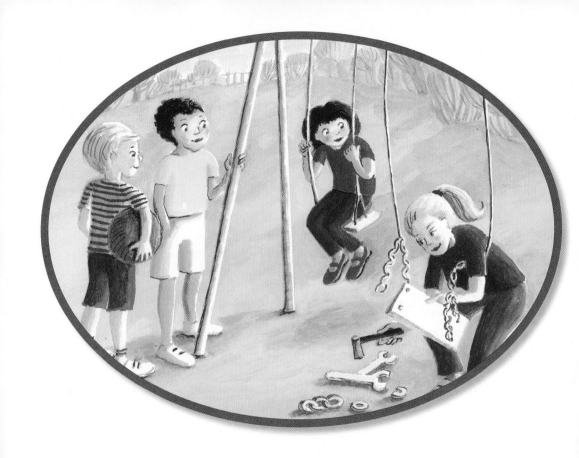

You can fix the swing.

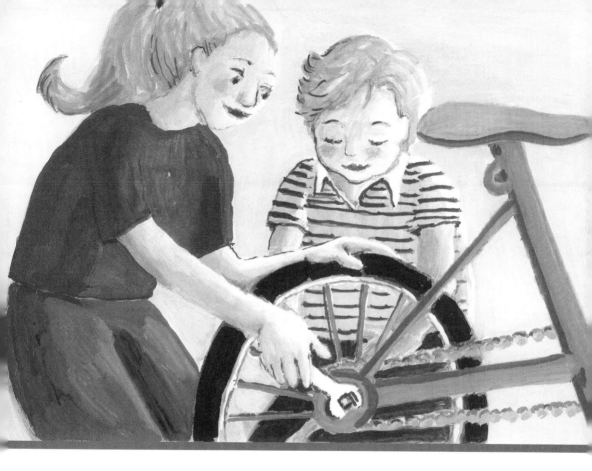

You can fix the bike.

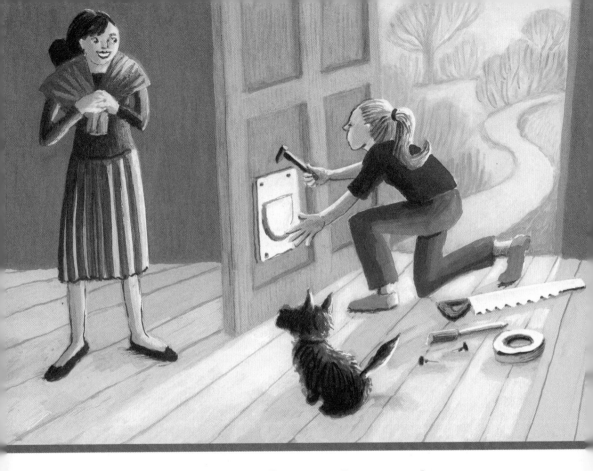

You can fix the door.

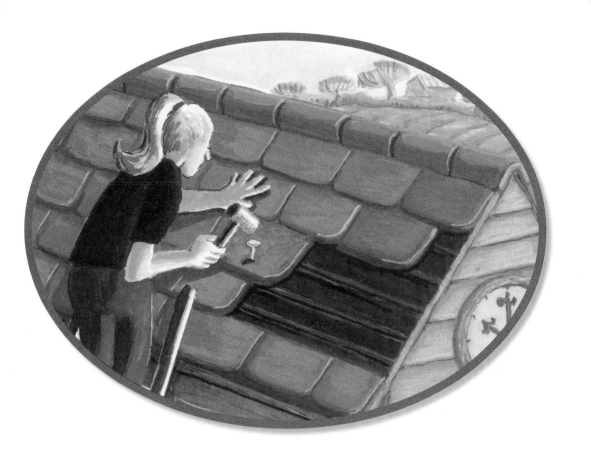

You can fix the roof.

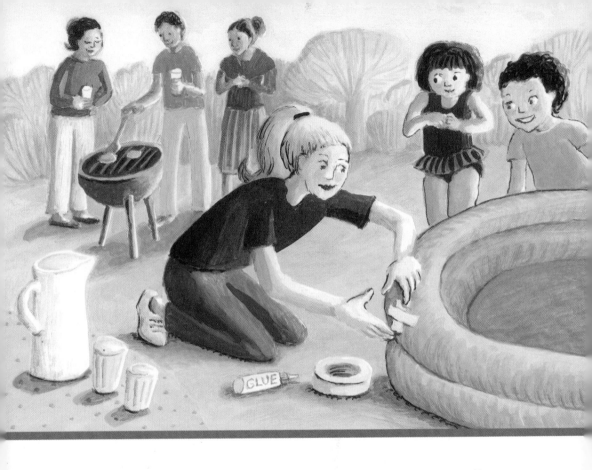

You can fix the pool.